Intimate Questions

459 Ways to Bring You Closer

Gregory J.P. Godek

CASABLANCA PRESS®
A DIVISION OF SOURCEBOOKS, INC.®
NAPERVILLE, ILLINOIS

Published by Sourcebooks, Inc.
P.O. Box 4410, Naperville, Illinois 60567-4410
(630) 961-3900
FAX: (630) 961-2168

Library of Congress Cataloging-in-Publication Data
Godek, Gregory J.P., 1955-
    Intimate Questions: 459 ways to bring you closer/Gregory Godek.
    p. cm.
    ISBN 1-57071-727-3 (alk. paper)
    1. Man-woman relationships—Miscellanea. 2. Intimacy
    (Psychology)—Miscellania I. Title.

HQ801 .G5546 2001
306.7—dc21

00-052653

Printed and bound in the United States of America.
PX 10 9 8 7 6 5 4 3 2 1

Dedication

To everyone who questions. To lovers who seek the depths of their relationships. To everyone who questions the status quo.
And, to the childlike quality in you that questions everything.
And, of course, to my Bride, Tracey—who answered "Yes!"
when I asked her the most important question I've ever asked anyone.

Contents

Introduction

A book of questions should begin with questions, don't you think?

Why did you buy this book? What do you hope to discover about yourself? What do you hope to learn about your partner? Are you seeking a method for exploring yourself and your relationship? If so, this book is designed specifically as a tool to help you on your path of discovery.

Questions are powerful. Questions are tools. Questions can be points of leverage. Questions can challenge your assumptions and beliefs. Questions lead to answers!

Some of the questions in this book are deceptively simple. Some are familiar—but deserve revisiting. Some may be shocking. But all of them are designed to help you understand yourself, your partner, and your relationship.

So, why don't we get started?!

Gregory J.P. Godek

Partnership

We partner up, two-by-two, automatically.
Human beings seem to function better in pairs.
This does NOT mean, however, that it's going to be easy!

1

What are the three best things about your partner?

2

What made you fall in love with your partner?

3

What do you and your partner usually argue about?

A Question of Balance

Successful couples are good at balancing their needs,
wants, and different personalities.

4

How do you balance your needs with your partner's needs?

5

How do you balance the needs of your relationship with
each of your individual needs?

6

How do you balance family and friends? Kids and spouse?
Yourself and your partner?

7

How do you balance work and play? Your strengths and weaknesses?

8

How do you balance the realities of your life today with
your dreams and visions?

9

How do you balance your personal life, professional life, and social life?

10

How do you balance your emotional, physical, and spiritual needs?

11

How do you balance your short-term needs and your long-term goals?

12

Just how important is balance, anyway?

Battle of the Sexes

The last time I checked, men and women weren't at war.
Let's declare "peace" in the Battle of the Sexes, okay?

13

What is the most mysterious thing about the opposite sex?

14

What's wrong with men? What's wrong with women?

15

Have you ever been infatuated? Describe the feeling.
Describe the relationship.

16

Do you consider yourself/your attitudes/your beliefs to be
fairly typical for your gender?

17

What is the one thing that the opposite gender simply
doesn't "get" about your gender?

18

What could members of the opposite sex learn by listening to you?

19

If you were going to write a self-help relationship book,
what would you title it?

20

Are there any circumstances in which it would be appropriate for a
man to physically strike a woman?

21

What was your most embarrassing moment in the
presence of a member of the opposite sex?

Beliefs

How your life unfolds is largely the result of the things you believe. (Do you believe this?)

22

Do you believe in love at first sight?

23

Do you believe in karma?

24

Do you believe in an afterlife? In heaven? In hell? In reincarnation?

25

Do you believe in astrology? Tarot? Palmistry?

26

Do you believe in the religion you were raised in?

27

Do you believe that two people can be "soul mates"?

28

Do you believe that the Bible is the inspired word of God? Do you believe it literally—or do you believe it's open to interpretation?

29

Do you believe it's proper for people to express their feelings in public?

30

Do you believe that people learn from their mistakes?

31

Do you believe that blondes have more fun?

32

Do you believe in the "American Dream"? (What is the "American Dream"?)

Business as Usual

What is your "world view"? How do your views coincide with and differ from those of your partner?

33

Do you believe that most politicians are dishonest?

34

Do you believe that most people are honest?

35

Should smoking tobacco be
banned? Should smoking marijuana be legalized?

36

Should handguns be licensed? Should toy guns be banned?

37

What is the biggest mistake your boss has made lately? If you were in
charge, what changes would you make?

What If . . .

*What if…you were to suspend your critical mind
and cynicism—and just "let yourself go"?!*

38

What if you had to tell the absolute truth for one solid week?

39

What if you could be a comic strip character…who would you be?

40

What if blue smoke came out of your ears every time
you became sexually aroused in the least little bit?

#1

What if you could create the absolute, perfect job for yourself...
what would it be?

Change

You will experience lots of change in any long-term relationship.
Don't let it take you by surprise!

#2

How does change happen in your life?
Are there any patterns that may be significant?

43

Is change sudden and dramatic?
Or does it happen slowly, more like an evolutionary process?

44

What kind of change do you face most calmly?
What kind of change is most emotional for you?

45

How have you changed for the better?
How have you changed for the worse?

46

Do you change? Or do things change around you?

47

What was the single most significant turning point in your life?

48

What person has helped you change for the better?

49

What book, movie, song, play, etc., has
helped you change for the better?

50

How do you handle unpredictable situations?

51

How do you think your life will change most
dramatically in the next five years? Ten years? Twenty years?

Clarifications

It helps if the two of you are "talking the same language." There's no absolute "right" and "wrong"—so let's clarify a few terms.

52

What is the difference between love, romance, and sex?

53

What is the difference between sexuality and sensuality?

54

What is the difference between having sex and making love?

Wishes

Wishing on a star is a good first step—it clarifies your dreams and desires. The second step is to crystalize those dreams into realistic goals.

55

If you had three wishes, what would they be? (And no, you cannot wish for an infinite number of wishes! Don't be greedy.)

56

You can instantly become a virtuoso musician on one instrument. What instrument is it?

57

What do you wish for your children?

58

You've suddenly become the most eloquent, talented public speaker of this generation... and you're about to address a crowd of 50,000 in Yankee Stadium. What is the message you're going to deliver?

Could You....?

Do you know what your capabilities are? It's wise to know your limitations; it's exhilarating to push your limits.

59

Could you run five miles right now?

60

Could you survive alone in the wilderness for a week?

61

Could you kill a person if you had to?

62

Could you live for a year in a tent with your partner?
(Without going crazy?!)

63

Could you change jobs and move to a
different city to be with your mate?

Do You....?

Your beliefs are a key to your personality. They affect your everyday behavior and how you treat your partner.

64

Do you expect that things will generally turn out for the best?

65

Do you vote?

66

Do you believe in God?

67

Do you take good enough care of yourself?

68

Do you often rethink your decisions,
or are you always certain that you're right?

Do You Agree?

*What is your "Philosophy of Life"? One way of getting a handle on it is to
see if you agree or disagree with the following statements.*

69

Absence makes the heart grow fonder.

70

Money makes the world go 'round.

71

It's not whether you win or lose, it's how you play the game.

72

All you need is love.

73

It is better to give than to receive.

74

You reap what you sow.

Dreams

Some people have big dreams. Others just dream their lives away.
How do you deal with your dreams?

75

What is your favorite daydream?
(Sexual fantasies don't count for this question!)

76

What is your dream job? What company? What role? What
industry? What product or service?

77

What is your dream home? Where? Why?

78

What is your dream vacation? Where? How long? What activities?

Either, Or

Either, or; this or that; now or then. There's no right or wrong (or is there?!)—just your opinion. Either way, your partner deserves to knows more about you!

79

Are you a peacekeeper or a troublemaker?

80

Are you a cat person or a dog person?

81

Are you outspoken or quiet?

82

Are you humble or arrogant?

83

Are you an outdoors person or a homebody?

84

Are you open or secretive?

Erotic

Sure, it's difficult talking about these
intimate issues, but let's give it a try…

85

What is the difference between sexy and erotic?

86

What is the most erotic movie scene you've ever seen?

87

What words do you want to hear during lovemaking?

88

What are the two most sensitive areas of your body?

89

How would you like your partner to dress during lovemaking?

Fame

*This is not the time to be modest. Do you feel comfortable
sharing your secret desires with your partner?*

90

You're going to be written up in *Who's Who.*
What will you be famous for?

91

If you could accomplish one crazy stunt that would land you in the
Guinness Book of World Records, what would it be?

92

If your name were to appear in the dictionary,
how would you define yourself?

93

The editors of *Bartlett's Familiar Quotations* want to include the quote
that you're most famous for. What is it?

Family Ties

A great deal of your personality was formed by your family.
So let's take a closer look…

94

How are you just like your father? Your mother?

95

Do you like the town you grew up in? Describe it.

96

What is your fondest memory from childhood?

97

What is your worst memory from childhood?

98

What were you like as a teenager?

99

When's the last time you called your mom,
just to tell her you love her? Your dad?

Favorite Things

*The better you know your partner, the better you'll be able
to find, buy, or create appropriate gifts.*

100

What is your favorite color?

101

What is your favorite number?

102

What is your favorite movie? Actor? Actress? Comedy? Drama?

103

What is your favorite dinner? Snack food?
Fancy restaurant? Fast food restaurant? Dessert?

104

What is your favorite comic strip? Comic character? TV cartoon?

Would You. . . ?

Would you take the time to answer a few questions for your lover?

105

Would you ever go skinny-dipping? With your partner in private?
With a group of other people?

106

Would you pick up a hitchhiker?

107

Would you ever run for a political office?

108

Would you give money to a homeless person?

109

If you were being mugged, would you fight,
run, or just give them your wallet?

Feelings

Okay, let's get down to it. Let's try some creative ways of expressing our feelings.

110

What movie or TV scene last brought tears to your eyes?

111

What feeling do you have the most difficulty controlling?

112

What feeling do you have the most difficulty expressing?

113

When is the last time you wrote a love letter?

114

What makes you feel most vulnerable?

115

When do you feel most fully engaged in living?

116

What do you do when you feel blue?

117

What makes you sad? Depressed?

118

What makes you ecstatic? Joyful?

119

When do you feel quietly at peace?

120

What feelings were your parents most uncomfortable expressing?
How has this affected you?

121

How do you feel at midnight on New Year's Eve? Christmas
morning? Your birthday?

Food, Glorious Food

Is the way to his heart through his stomach? It's worth a try!
(This seems to work equally well for the women—take note, guys.)

122

What is the "Best Food In The World"?

123

When you sit down in front of a great movie, what junk food do you
want within arm's reach?

124

You can obliterate one kind of food from the face of the earth.
What food is it?

125

Are you a picky eater?

126

What is your favorite meal of the day: breakfast, lunch, or dinner?
Or snacks?!

For Marrieds Only

*To have and to hold, for better or for worse, from this day forward, I now
pronounce you husband and wife.*

127

Before anything was "official," how did you know you
were going to marry each other?

128

Where were you when you proposed (or were proposed to)?
Exactly what was said?

129

As you were growing up, what kind of person
did you imagine you'd marry?

130

What is the funniest/most embarrassing/most touching thing
that happened during your wedding?

131

Do you believe that you and your spouse were destined to be together?

For Marrieds Only

Part II

The happiest married couples are those who don't take each other for grant-ed—those who cherish each other in words and actions.

132

How do you plan to celebrate your 50th wedding anniversary?

133

What are your goals as a couple? How are your goals
for yourself supported by your marriage?

134

Do you want any (more) children?

135

Should husband and wife be each other's best friend?

For Men Only

Okay, guys, listen up! I know you sometimes have difficulty expressing your feelings. But we all know they're in there…

136

What's the best thing about being male?

137

What's the worst thing about being male?

138

Do you feel misunderstood by women?

139

What is your least masculine attribute?
Are you uncomfortable talking about it?

140

Which are you more afraid of: cancer or impotence?

141

Ideally, how often would you like to have sex?

For Singles Only

*Dating shouldn't be about impressing the other person
but about getting him or her to know you better.*

142

Can you list twenty-five qualities of your perfect partner?

143

How old do you expect to be when you get married?

144

Assuming you won't find a partner who is 100 percent
perfect, what specific characteristics must your
partner possess, and which could you live without?

145

How important is it that the person you marry
share your religious beliefs?

146

Do you want to have children? How many? Boys or girls? When?

147

What is the best thing about being single?

148

What is the worst thing about being single?

149

What aspect of the single life would you like
to carry over into your married life?

150

What is the minimum length of time two people
should date before getting engaged?

151

How do your life values compare
with your partner's? How do your sexual values compare?

For Women Only

Do you think that women are the "fairer sex"?
What do you really want men to understand about women?

152

What is the best thing about being a woman?

153

What is the worst thing about being a woman?

154

Do you experience PMS?
How do you want to be treated during your period?

155

What is your most masculine trait?
Do you use it, or do you tend to suppress it?

156

Do you feel misunderstood by men?

157

Are you a feminist?

Fun and Games

Getting in touch with your "inner child" is one thing, but getting him or her to come out and play is another!

158

What was your favorite game as a child?

159

What is your favorite game now?

160

Do you like crossword puzzles? Jigsaw puzzles? Brainteasers?

161

What would you like to learn how to do?
(Play guitar? Sail? Learn a new language? Meditate?)

Getting Down to Business

*You'll spend a third to half of your waking hours at work.
What are your attitudes toward work? How will your work
habits affect your relationship?*

162

Do you earn what you're worth?

163

Do top corporate executives earn too much money?

164

Should lobbying in Congress be outlawed?

165

Are there too many lawyers?

166

Do doctors earn too much money?
Government workers? Union members? Teachers?

Getting to Know You

*Deep down we all want the same thing:
to be known, understood, and appreciated.*

167

Which three nouns best describe you? Which three adjectives?

168

Which period of your life did you enjoy the most? Childhood?
Adolescence? Young adulthood? Adulthood? Right now?

169

What do you want to be remembered for?

170

Who are you? (How do you define yourself?)

Survivor

Some of these "crazy" questions can reveal important insights into your personality, values, and dreams.

If you were stranded on a desert island...

171

What food would you miss the most?

172

What three music albums/CDs would you most like to have?

173

Would you wear clothes?

174

What three books would you take along?

175

What one person would you want to be there with you?

Ha-ha-ha-ha-ha!

People in happy, long-term relationships know that when all else fails, their sense of humor sees them through.

176

What's your favorite joke?

177

What's the funniest thing you've ever said?

178

What's the funniest thing you've ever done?

179

What's the funniest thing that's ever happened to you?

180

What's the best practical joke you've ever pulled?

181

When have you been doubled over with laughter?

History

Here are some exercises in creative fantasy. Playing the question game of "What if…" can be quite insightful.

182

If you could become one historical figure, who would it be? Would you change anything about the way he or she lived his or her life?

183

What are the five greatest achievements of humankind?

184

If you could have stopped one war from occurring, which one would it be? Why?

185

You can go back and participate in the writing of the U.S. Constitution. You can add one new item to the Bill of Rights. What is it?

Hmmm?

How often do you take time to ponder what makes you tick? Curiosity about yourself—and your partner—is a characteristic of life-long lovers.

186

What makes you jealous?

187

What makes you angry?

188

What makes you sad?

189

Did you read *The Bridges of Madison County*?
Did Francesca do the right thing?

190

Which is more important: education or experience?

191

How often do you call your parents?

Huh?

*Questions about little, seemingly insignificant facets of your
personality may actually shed the most light on who you are.*

192

Do you fold your underwear or just stuff it in the drawer?

193

At what age will you let your children date?

194

Would you rather go to Mardi Gras
in New Orleans, or New Year's Eve in Times Square?

195

Would you rather go to the Moon or to Mars?

196

What three famous living people would you like to be friends with?

Yikes!

Do you like a good scare? A good surprise?
Do you like roller coasters? Do you like surprise birthday parties?

197

What's the luckiest thing that's ever happened to you?

198

What's the weirdest or creepiest thing that's ever happened to you?

199

Can you sing the theme song to
The Flintstones? The Brady Bunch? The Jetsons? Gilligan's Island?
The Partridge Family? The Addams Family? Your favorite TV show?

200

Who is in charge of the TV remote control in your relationship?

201

What activity do you like to do that's "on the edge"?

If

This isn't just idle dreaming…it's a door to your secret dreams and desires.
Will you share them with your partner?

202

If you could be any age for a day, what age would you be?

203

If you could change one thing about your parents, what would it be?
How would you be different now if that change
had been made when you were a child?

204

If you had one million dollars that you had to give away,
who or what would you give it to?

205

If you could become invisible for a week, what would you do?

206

If you ran Mattel Toy Company, what new toys would you create?

207

If you were head of the United Nations, how would
you try to promote world peace?

208

If you could organize all of your days to suit your
personality perfectly, what would each 24-hour period look like?

209

If you could be any height and weight, what would they be?

Kid Stuff

A lot of your behavior today is based on your experiences during the first ten years of your life. How much do you remember of that time?

210

What was your favorite toy when you were young?

211

Did you ever have a nickname?

212

Did you have a favorite pet when you were a kid?

213

Who was your "Very Best Friend" at various ages?
What are your best memories of your times together?
Where are they now?

214

How many brothers and sisters do you have?
Do you think your birth order has affected your personality?

Memories

Do you remember when life was simpler, less complicated?
(Or does it only seem that way?!)

215

Do you remember your very first kiss?

216

Who was your very first girlfriend or boyfriend?

217

What one thing did your parents always yell at you for?

218

What did you get away with in high school that you've
still never told anyone about?

219

What is your earliest memory of childhood?

Miscellaneous

*Unusual questions challenge your normal ways of thinking;
they challenge your assumptions. Therefore, they help to
reveal who you really are.*

220

You can create one new national holiday. What is it called,
what does it celebrate, and on what date does it fall?

221

You can choose new parents. Who are they?

222

What one part of your body would you change?

223

How many years would you like to live?

224

What would you like your epitaph to read?

225

What animal would you like to be?

226

Who would you like to punch in the nose?

227

What one bad habit would you like to change?

228

What one good habit would you like to start?

229

Who is your best friend in all the world?

230

God wants an even dozen instead of only ten Commandments.
What are the two new Commandments?

Who Are You?

Sometimes the simplest, most basic questions are the most revealing.

231

How would your best friend describe you?

232

How would your worst enemy describe you?

233

Whose ego is more fragile—yours or your partner's?

Who Asked You?

*One would think that answering questions about one's self
would be easy to do. After all, you've lived with yourself
all your life! Curious, isn't it?*

234

What book have you been meaning to read?

235

Where in the world have you always wanted to visit?

236

If you were a member of the opposite sex, what would your name be?

Very Interesting

Letting yourself be known—really known—by another person takes time, understanding, patience, and trust.

237

Do you tend to have "good luck" or "bad luck"?

238

Are your "hunches" usually right? How often do you act on them?

239

If you were Rick, in the movie *Casablanca*,
would you have let Ilsa (Ingrid Bergman) leave at the end?

What?!

Do you consider yourself to be creative? Is creativity a part of your everyday life? Did you know that the most romantic couples are creatively romantic?

240

When do you feel most creative?
During what activities are you most creative?

241

If you had just one more day to live, what would you do?

242

If you had just six more months to live, what would you do?

Goals

Do you set goals for yourself? Do you write them down?
How do you celebrate when you accomplish them?

243

What five accomplishments are you most proud of?

244

What are your three top goals for this year?

245

What are your top ten goals for your lifetime?

246

If you could change one decision you've made
in your life, what would it be?

If You Were King

Have you ever said, "What fools! If only I were king (queen) of the world, I'd fix things so they'd work better!" I can't crown you—but I can give you the opportunity to express your opinions:

247

Would the world be better off without money? Taxes? TV? Religion? The opposite sex? The Pill? Computers? Rock music? Rap music? Opera? Football? Cars? Fundamentalists? Conservatives? Liberals? Spiders? *Playboy* magazine? Nuclear weapons? Welfare? Cigarettes? Farm subsidies? Congress? Credit cards? Video games? Handguns? Lawyers? Talk shows? Speed limits? The Internet? Advertising? TV weather reporters? Mandatory schooling? Communism? Capitalism? Socialism? The Academy Awards? Daily newspapers? Fast food? So many cookbooks? Therapists? Advice columnists? The common cold? Drugs? Chocolate? Cell phones?

Money

Studies show that couples fight about money more than any other issue. You don't need to see eye-to-eye, but you'll get along much better if you understand each other's attitudes about money.

248

You've just been given one million dollars (tax free). What is the first thing you'll do tomorrow morning?

249

You just found a wallet with $500 cash in it. What will you do with it?

250

You have two million dollars to spend specifically on a collection of some kind. What would you buy?

251

If you're so smart, why aren't you a millionaire?

252

Would you ever spend $300 on a bottle of wine?

253

How much tip do you give in restaurants? To taxi drivers?
To hotel attendants? To a waiter who's given you lousy service?

254

Should taxes be reduced? Should rich people pay more taxes?

255

What is your definition of "rich"?

More Money

Do you feel better when you have money in the bank?
Do you feel good about the way you earn money?

256

Are you good or bad with money?

257

Are you a big spender or a cheapskate?

259

Should couples have joint or individual bank accounts?

259

How many credit cards do you have? Why?

260

Which would be worse: losing your wallet or
being embarrassed in public?

261

Do you believe that love of money is the root of evil?

More or Less

Let's face it, we all compare ourselves with others.
We can't help it...so let's at least be honest about it!

262

Are you more or less ambitious than your coworkers?

263

Are you more or less spiritual than your partner?

264

Are you more or less intelligent than most people?

265

Are you more or less sensitive than most people?

266

Are you more or less moral than most people?

267

Are you more or less sensual than most people?

268

Are you more or less mature than most people?

269

Are you more or less thoughtful than most people?

270

Are you more or less competitive than most people?

271

Are you more or less healthy than most people?

272

Are you more or less emotionally stable than most people?

Movie Inspired Questions

*Movies have always explored the questions of love.
Do you agree with their conclusions? What do you think of the
movies' portrayal of love? Of men? Of women?*

273

Can men and women be just friends?
(*When Harry Met Sally*)

274

What is your quest? (*Monty Python and the Holy Grail*)

275

Would you sleep with a stranger for one million dollars?
(*Indecent Proposal*)

276

Is there one perfect person for everyone? (*Sleepless In Seattle*)

Musical Interludes

Music has been called the "Language of Love."
Do you agree? How do you use music to express your love?

277

Your favorite singer is writing a song about you.
What's the title of the song? Sing it.

278

What is your favorite type of music? Favorite singer?
Favorite musical group?

279

What is your favorite song? Favorite dance tune?
Favorite ballad? Favorite classical piece? Favorite love song?

280

Did your parents sing you to sleep at night?
What songs did they sing?

Nighty-Night

You'll spend a quarter to a third of your life in bed.
So let's make the most of it!

281

Are you a sound sleeper?

282

Do you remember your dreams? Do you dream in color?

283

Do you have to sleep on the same side of the bed all the time?

284

What is your favorite position in which to fall asleep with your partner: spoons, bookends, pretzels, or something else?

Okay?

*Your values are reflected in the kinds of things you approve
of and disapprove of. What kinds of issues are you adamant about,
and what kinds are you flexible on?*

285

Is it okay for people of different races to date?
To marry? To have children?

286

Is it okay for your partner to have a best friend—of the opposite sex?

287

Is it okay to lie under certain circumstances? What's the
difference between a "little white lie" and other kinds of lies?

288

Is it okay to lie to avoid hurting someone's feelings?

One Day at a Time

Personally, I have a hard time grasping the time frame of a year. It's such a lot of time! A month is long, too. Weeks are okay…but a day—one day at a time—is just the right amount of time. I can deal with that. How about you?

289

What holiday do you most look forward to every year?
What holiday or event do you dread the most?

290

What are your most and least favorite days of the week?
Why? What could you do to ease the pain?

291

If you had one extra hour each day, what would you do with it?
If you had one extra day each week, what would you do with it?

People

How many people do you like to be with? Many, like at a party?
A few, like at an intimate get-together? Just the two of you?
Or do you prefer to be alone?

292

If you could have a conversation with one famous person in
history, who would it be? What would you talk about?

293

If you could talk with a fictional person, who would it be?

294

Who are the three greatest people in history?

295

Do you know someone who really
needs your advice? What advice would you give him/her?

296

Who are the people for whom you would do anything?

Perfect

Nobody's perfect—but the idea of what you consider to be perfect/ultimate/awesome tells us a lot about you.

297

What's your idea of the "Perfect Date"?

298

What would the "Perfect Weekend" consist of?

299

What's your idea of the "Perfect Kiss"?

300

What would "Perfect Sex" be like?

301

What would the "Perfect Vacation" be like?

Philosophy 101

You may not think of yourself as a "philosopher," but everyone has a "philosophy of life"—a set of beliefs that guide our actions; a view of life that explains why things are the way they are.

302

Why does the world exist?

303

How did the universe begin?

304

What one book should everyone in the world be required to read?

305

What is your philosophy of life?

306

Is there one phrase that sums up your philosophy?

Power

They say that power corrupts. Do you think you could wield power well and responsibly? How do you handle power in your life right now?

307

If you were President of the United States of America, what's the first thing you would do?

308

If you were the Pope, what would you do?

309

Who has more power in our society, men or women? Who has more power in your relationship, you or your partner?

310

If you ran the nation's school system, what changes would you make?

Psychological Stuff

Do you know what's going on inside your head? Do you know what's going on inside your lover's head? You might want to look into it!

311

What motivates you to do your best?

312

How do you handle uncertainty?

313

What are you afraid of? (Fear of failure? Rejection?
Abandonment? Your own anger? Others' anger? Inadequacy?)

314

Under what circumstance would you seek the help of a counselor or
therapist for yourself? Would you consider seeing a couples' counselor
if your partner felt it was necessary?

315

What do you feel is your life's central emotional challenge?
Intellectual challenge? Career challenge?

Yin and Yang

The world, our lives, and our relationships are in constant flux.
Energy ebbs and flows. We are all different—yet the same.
How do you deal with it all?!

316

What do you believe is the biggest
difference between men and women?

317

Do you believe that opposites
attract? Do you think that's a good basis for a loving relationship?

318

Do you tend to see things as black and white, or as shades of gray?

319

How consistent are your actions with your beliefs?
How do you handle your own inconsistencies?

320

What lessons should be learned from children? From senior citizens?

Romance

Do you have enough romance in your life right now?
How important is romance in your life?

321

What is the most romantic thing you've ever done?

322

What is the most romantic thing that's ever been done for you?

323

Have you ever had a broken heart? How long did it take to heal?

324

How do you define "Romance"?

325

Who's more romantic, men or women? Why do you suppose this is?

Say It

We all keep a lot of things inside: feelings, longings, resentments, desires. Sometimes it's good to express them. Sometimes simply acknowledging them is enough.

326

What would you like to say to your father but just haven't been able to say?

327

What would you like to say to your mother? Your brothers or sisters?

328

What do you wish you could say to your boss, but you don't because you'd probably get fired?

329

Have you ever said anything that you wish you could take back?

School Daze

Did you like school? Were you a member of the "in" crowd?
Did you study much? Did you worry about school?

330

What was your best subject in grade school? High school? College?

331

What was your worst subject?

332

Who was your best teacher? What did he or she teach you?

333

You can go back and change one thing that happened to you in high school. What would you change—and how would this affect your life today?

334

Do you remember your first school dance? Your third grade teacher? Your worst experience in gym class?

Science Fiction

Technology advances, science expands the frontiers of knowledge, but human nature remains the same: we'll always be struggling with the mysteries of love.

335

Which would you rather have:
a time machine or a matter transfer device?

336

Which *Star Trek* series is best?

337

If you had access to a holodeck (like they have on *Star Trek: The Next Generation*), how would you use it?

338

Which would you rather explore: outer space,
the ocean depths, or the psychic frontier?

Secrets

*Skeletons in the closet?!—Who me? Not me! No way! What would
make you think such a thing? (Well, maybe there was this one time…)*

339

Have you ever told something to a stranger on a
plane that you haven't told your partner?

340

Have you ever cheated in school? On your taxes?

341

Are there any family secrets that you carry with you?

Intimate Fantasies

Kids know how to fantasize without being taught. We adults have to relearn how to let our imaginations run wild again.

342

What is your secret sexual fantasy?
(You know, that one that you've never shared with anyone.)

343

Where would you like to have sex?

344

Ideally, how often would you like to have sex?

345

What kind of clothing do you find sexy?

346

What kind of lingerie do you prefer?

Foreplay

Here's where we're really going to uncover some assumptions between the two of you. Hang in there!

347

Do you know what your partner's favorite foreplay activity is?

348

What is your favorite foreplay activity? To give? To receive?

349

Can you describe an orgasm? (What color is it? Does it tingle, explode, flow? Does it linger? How long? How else would you describe it?)

350

Do you feel comfortable asking your
partner for specific kinds of stimulation?

Sex

*As a culture, we are obsessed with sex.
And yet we rarely really talk about it.*

351

Would you rather be rich or sexy?

352

Would you like to have sex outside?
Would you do it if your partner wanted to?

353

Would you ever have sex in an elevator?
What outrageous location would excite you?

354

Would you like to join the Mile High Club?

355

Have you ever had sex in your living room?
In the laundry room? On the kitchen table?

356

How has your sexuality changed over the years?

357

What sexual activity have you never before done but would like to try?

358

If your children are sexually active at the same age that you were, will that be okay with you?

Hot Stuff!

What are your personal turn-ons? You don't have to tell all of us—just your very own intimate partner.

359

Have you ever made love in the back seat of a car?

360

What are your favorite erotic and/or sexy movies?

361

Would you like your lover to be more sexually assertive?
How—specifically?

362

What songs make you think of making love? Do you own them?

363

How did you first learn about sex?
What crazy misconceptions did you once have?

Simply Outrageous!

There is a time and a place for acting mature and grown up.
But it's not always and everywhere! What is the most
wild/outrageous part of your personality?

364

You can commit one crime and get away with it completely.
What would that crime be?

365

If you could be a superhero, who would you be?

366

If you could be a new superhero (with new powers),
what would you call yourself, and what would your powers be?

367

If you were going to get a tattoo, what would it be?
Where on your body would it be?

Smarty Pants!

*There are many ways of being "smart"—just as there are
many ways of being romantic.*

368

Would you rather be really, really smart, or really, really good looking?

369

How are you smart? What are your best talents?

370

Are your decisions usually right?

371

If you had an IQ of 190, how would it change your life?

Stuff

You're surrounded by stuff. Some of it is yours, some of it belongs to others, and some of it you share. How do you and your partner deal with your stuff?

372

What's your favorite stuff? (What are your favorite possessions?)

373

What was your favorite stuff when you were a baby?
A child? An adolescent?

374

What do you carry in your pockets?
In your purse? In your briefcase?

375

What is the single most expensive item you own?

376

What personal item do you value the most?

Supercalifragilisticexpialidocious

Does everything have to make sense?
How imaginative are you?

377

What are the three greatest inventions of all time?

378

Would you rather have the power to become
invisible or the power to levitate things?

379

If you could have great talent in one area, which would
you choose: writing, art, or music? Why?

Time

Think about it: time is your most precious resource of all. Do you use it wisely? How much of it do you spend on your relationship?

380

If you could save time in a bottle, what would you do with it?
(Thank you, Jim Croce.)

381

What is your favorite time of day?

382

What is your favorite season?

383

If there were eight days in a week,
what would you do with that extra day?

384

How many minutes of undivided attention
per day do you give your partner?

Togetherness

It seems to be human nature to want to "couple-up."
Maybe it's true that two heads are better than one!

385

Can a person be too much in love?

386

Can you read your partner's mind?

387

If you could dress your partner, how would you dress him/her?

388

Is your lover your best friend?

389

What is the best relationship advice you've ever gotten?

Potpourri

*Your thoughts, opinions, and unique points-of-view
make you who you are. Who are you?*

390

Do you have a guardian angel?

391

Do you have neat handwriting?
What does your signature reveal about your personality?

392

Are you happy with your name?
If you could, what would you change it to?

TV

It's said that the average American watches seven hours of TV per day! What are your TV habits?

393

A new TV sitcom is going to be created, based on your life. What is the name of the show? Describe the major characters. What is the basic plot?

394

Oprah is going to devote a whole show to you. Complete this phrase: "Next, on *Oprah*, (_____)."

395

What, in your opinion, is the "Greatest TV Show In The World"? Why?

396

What TV show are you embarrassed to admit that you enjoy?

Part II

The Boob Tube; the Great American Invention;
the One-Eyed Monster. Has it eaten your brain?
Do you spend as much time with your partner as with the TV?

397

How many hours of TV do you watch in an average day?

398

Is there too much violence on TV? Too much sex?

399

You've just been made president of NBC.
What changes would you make?

400

The TV show 60 *Minutes* is going to do an exposé on you.
What skeletons have they discovered in your closet?
How will you respond?

Your Life

*It's your life. You're in charge. You get to make
all the decisions. Cool, huh?*

401

Who is your mentor? Hero? Role model?

402

Barbara Walters is going to interview you for TV.
What are her first three questions to you?

403

They're going to make a movie about your life. What kind of movie is
it? (Comedy? Tragedy? Adventure? Science fiction? Romance?)
What is the title of the movie? Who stars in it? Who plays you?

404

Imagine that your life is a story—a novel—and you are the author.
What is the title of this novel? What chapter are you now living?
What kind of story are you going to write (live)
over the next ten, twenty, thirty, forty years?

Weird Science

Let your imagination run wild…where will it lead you?

#05

If you could change one of the Laws of Physics,
which one would it be? What would the new law be?

#06

If you could live in the past, what year would you go to,
and what location would you go to?

#07

If you could live in the future, what year would you go to,
and what location would you go to?

#408

If you had been the first person on the Moon,
what would you have said as you stepped onto the surface?

You!

*Let's get personal. These questions tap into some private parts of
your personality. Are you willing to share them?*

#409

Would you rather be rich or famous?

#410

If you could save just one object
from your burning home, what would it be?

#11

What is your very best quality? (This is not the time to be modest.)

#12

What is your very worst quality? What is the dark side of your personality? (How do you deal with it? Ignore it? Fight it? Give in to it? Harness it?)

#13

Are you open-minded? (Does your partner agree?)

#14

What traditions are important to you? (Family traditions? Religious traditions? Holiday traditions?)

#15

If you had to be either blind or deaf, which would you choose?

#16

What is your most cherished photo?

#17

Who do you need to forgive?

You Two

*This is about you. And about your partner, too.
The two of you. The more you know about each other,
the deeper your love can grow.*

#18

What makes you nostalgic? Homesick? Thoughtful?

#19

What gives you the creeps?

#20

What makes you horny?

#421

What fascinates you?

#422

How is your relationship the same as your parents'? How is it different?

#423

If your partner had an affair, could you forgive him or her?

#424

Were the two of you "made for each other"?

#425

How did you know when the two of you had become a "couple"?

Miscellany

There are many, many facets to your personality.
Worth a lifetime of inquiry.

426

What did you want to be when you grew up?

427

If men instead of women had babies, how would the world be different?

428

Right this minute—as you are reading this—how is your health?
Are you in love? What emotions are you feeling? Do you wish you
were doing something else? Do you feel happy?

Opposites

Opposites attract, right? Sometimes yes, sometimes no.

429

How are you and your partner "opposites"?

430

How are you and your partner exactly the same?

431

What was the biggest fight you've ever had with
any member of the opposite sex?

432

When you were growing up, what was your relationship
like with your parent of the opposite sex?

433

Which of your character traits is the
most at odds with general cultural norms?

Generations

*Your early years have had a vast impact on who you are today. Family,
relatives, and close friends all leave their mark on us.*

434

Who is your favorite relative? Why?

435

Who is your least favorite relative? Why?

436

What life lesson did you learn from one of your grandparents?

437

What one wish do you have for your children?

438

What is your philosophy on raising children?

Dream On

Dreams are a mysterious phenomenon of our existence.
Every belief about them is just a theory. What do you think?

#39

Do you believe that dreams reveal your inner desires?
Are dreams a doorway to your unconscious mind?

#40

Do you believe that dreams can foretell the future?

#41

Do you remember any dreams from your childhood?

Fun, Fun, Fun!

While most of us don't really believe that our purpose on Earth is to have fun, it certainly makes being here more worthwhile.

442

What's the most fun you've ever had with your clothes on?

443

What's the most fun you've ever had with your clothes off?

444

When you were a kid, did you play with members of the opposite sex? Did you think boys/girls were "yucky"?

445

At what age did you start really being interested in the opposite sex?

446

Do you play enough now?

Think About It

Here are some things that, perhaps, you've never thought about.
Lucky you—now you have the opportunity!

447

If you went bald, would you wear a toupee?

#448

Would you ever go to a nude beach?

#449

What is your favorite planet?

#450

What is your favorite breed of dog? Cat?

#451

If you were going to appear on David Letterman's "Stupid Human Tricks" segment, what would you do?

Grades

We get graded in school, but from that point forward we rarely use an objective grading system to evaluate ourselves. It might help!

452

What grade would you give your relationship?
(Grade yourself like in school, A through F.)

453

What grade would you give your performance at work?

454

On a scale of 1 to 10, how good a secret-keeper are you?

#55

On a scale of 1 to 10, how skilled a lover are you?

Favorite Things

Part II

*You don't need to defend any of your choices
or preferences. They simply are.*

#56

What is your favorite song? Love song? Dance tune?
Classical composition? Instrumental piece?

#57

What is your favorite musical band?

#58

What is your favorite magazine?

#59

Who is your favorite comedian?

Also by Gregory J.P. Godek:

1001 Ways To Be Romantic
5th Anniversary Edition of the Bestselling Classic!

10,000 Ways to Say I Love You

Enchanted Evenings

LoveQuotes Coupons

I Love You Coupons

To order these books or any other of our many publications, please contact your local bookseller, gift store, or call Sourcebooks. Books by Gregory J.P. Godek are available in book and gift stores across North America. Get a copy of our catalog by writing or faxing:

Sourcebooks, Inc
P. O. Box 4410
Naperville, IL 60567-4410
(630) 961-3900
FAX: (630) 961-2168